-Mapographica-

the  NATURAL WORLD

JON RICHARDS *and* ED SIMKINS

 Crabtree Publishing Company
www.crabtreebooks.com

Crabtree Publishing Company
www.crabtreebooks.com
1-800-387-7650

Published in Canada	**Published in the United States**
Crabtree Publishing	**Crabtree Publishing**
616 Welland Avenue	PMB 59051
St. Catharines, ON	350 Fifth Ave, 59th Floor
L2M 5V6	New York, NY 10118

Published in 2017 by CRABTREE PUBLISHING COMPANY.

First published in 2015 by Wayland
(A division of Hachette Children's Books)
Copyright © Wayland 2015

Authors: Jon Richards, Ed Simkins
Editorial director: Kathy Middleton
Editors: Julia Adams, Jon Richards, and Ellen Rodger
Designer: Ed Simkins
Proofreaders: Wendy Scavuzzo, and Petrice Custance
Prepress technician: Tammy McGarr
Print and production coordinator: Katherine Berti

The publisher would like to thank the following for their kind permission to reproduce their photographs:

Key: (t) top; (c) center; (b) bottom; (l) left; (r) right

Cover front, 1br, 15r isotckphoto.com/Pavlo_K, cover back, 4-5 courtesy of NASA, 1tl, 4-5 light bulbs istockphoto.com/choness, 3c courtesy of NASA, 9br istockphoto.com/Daniel Barnes, 10-11 palm oil fruit istockphoto.com/nop16, 11l istockphoto.com/yotrak, 11br istockphoto.com/kjorgen, 12bl istockphoto.com/Olena Druzhynina, 14-15 istockphoto.com/David Sucsy, 15bc istockphoto.com, 21tr istockphoto.com/leungchopan, 21cr istockphoto.com/Chris Hepburn, 21br istockphoto.com/Xavier Arnau, 26-27 istockphoto.com/MillefloreImages, 27br istockphoto.com/tavor, 28-29 all courtesy of NASA, 30c istockphoto.com/nicoolay, 30cr istockphoto.com/Manakin

Every attempt has been made to clear copyright. Should there be any inadvertent omission, please apply to the publisher for rectification.

The website addresses (URLs) included in this book were valid at the time of going to press. However, it is possible that contents or addresses may have changed since the publication of this book. No responsibility for any such changes can be accepted by either the author or the Publisher.

Printed in Canada/072016/PB20160525

Library and Archives Canada Cataloguing in Publication

Richards, Jon, 1970-, author
    The natural world / Jon Richards, Ed Simkins.

(Mapographica: your world in infographics)
Includes index.
Issued in print and electronic formats.
ISBN 978-0-7787-2658-6 (hardback).--
ISBN 978-0-7787-2662-3 (paperback).--
ISBN 978-1-4271-1798-4 (html)

    1. Nature--Miscellanea--Juvenile literature. 2. Organisms--Miscellanea--Juvenile literature. 3. Natural history--Miscellanea--Juvenile literature. 4. Geology--Miscellanea--Juvenile literature. 5. Earth (Planet)--Miscellanea--Juvenile literature. I. Simkins, Ed, author II. Title.

QH48.R54 2016   j508   C2016-902669-8
                                     C2016-902670-1

Library of Congress Cataloging-in-Publication Data

Names: Richards, Jon, 1970- author. | Simkins, Ed, author.
Title: The natural world / Jon Richards and Ed Simkins.
Description: St. Catharines, Ontario ; New York, New York : Crabtree Publishing, 2017. | Series: Mapographica: your world in infographics | "First published in 2015 by Wayland." | Includes index.
Identifiers: LCCN 2016016683 (print) | LCCN 2016017067 (ebook) | ISBN 9780778726586 (reinforced library binding) | ISBN 9780778726623 (pbk.) | ISBN 9781427117984 (electronic HTML)
Subjects: LCSH: Nature--Miscellanea--Juvenile literature. | Natural history--Miscellanea--Juvenile literature. | Geology--Miscellanea--Juvenile literature. | Earth (Planet)--Miscellanea--Juvenile literature.
Classification: LCC QH48 .R52 2017 (print) | LCC QH48 (ebook) | DDC 508--dc23
LC record available at https://lccn.loc.gov/2016016683

CONTENTS

— Our natural Planet —

Earth is an ever-changing planet. Deep beneath its crust, churning molten rock pushes and pulls on the surface, creating volcanoes and earthquakes, and shaping the land. The planet is also home to a vast range of different ecosystems, from the dark ocean depths to the lush rain forests and freezing polar ice caps.

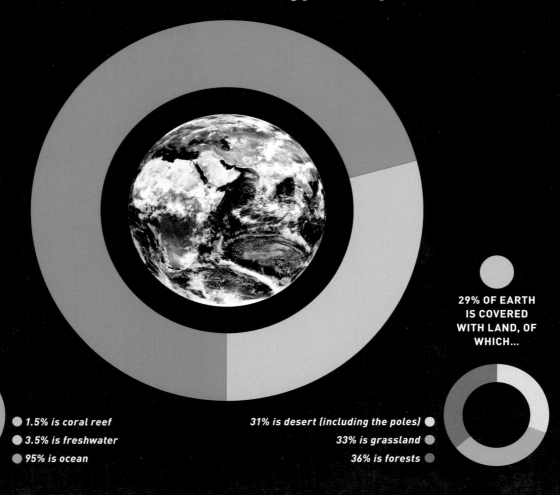

71% OF EARTH IS COVERED WITH WATER, OF WHICH...

29% OF EARTH IS COVERED WITH LAND, OF WHICH...

● 1.5% is coral reef
● 3.5% is freshwater
● 95% is ocean

31% is desert (including the poles) ●
33% is grassland ●
36% is forests ●

Our
PLANET

The world is divided into large landmasses called **continents**, and together these cover 57.5 million sq miles (148.9 million sq km), which is nearly 30 percent of Earth's total surface area. The continents feature towering peaks that stretch high into the sky, rivers that wind for thousands of miles, and large islands.

EUROPE
NORTH AMERICA
ASIA
AFRICA
SOUTH AMERICA
AUSTRALIA/ OCEANIA

NORTH AMERICA

Highest mountains

Denali
20,321 ft
(6,194 m)

Mt Logan
19,550 ft
(5,959 m)

Pico de Orizaba
18,490 ft
(5,636 m)

Longest rivers

Missouri 2,340 miles (3,766 km)

Mississippi 2,320 miles (3,734 km)

Yukon 1,980 miles (3,187 km)

Largest islands

Greenland
836,330 sq miles
(2,166,086 sq km)

Baffin
195,928 sq miles
(507,451 sq km)

Ellesmere
75,767 sq miles
(196,235 sq km)

SOUTH AMERICA

Highest mountains

Aconcagua
22,949 ft
(6,995 m)

Oyos del Salado
22,615 ft
(6,893 m)

Monte Pississ
22,287 ft
(6,793 m)

Longest rivers

Amazon 4,000 miles (6,437 km)

Paraná 3,032 miles (4,880 km)

Madeira 2,019 miles (3,250 km)

Largest islands

Isla Grande de Tierra del Fuego
95,753 sq miles
(248,000 sq km)

Marajó
15,483 sq miles
(40,100 sq km)

Chiloé
3,241 sq miles
(8,394 sq km)

EUROPE

Highest mountains

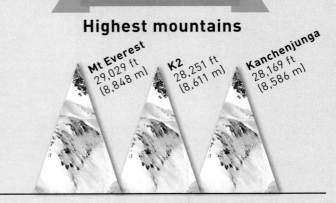

Elbrus 18,510 ft (5,642 m)

Kazbek 16,512 ft (5,033 m)

Mont Blanc 15,781 ft (4,810 m)

Longest rivers

Volga 2,294 miles (3,692 km)

Danube 1,777 miles (2,860 km)

Ural 1,509 miles (2,428 km)

Largest islands

Great Britain 88,759 sq miles (229,885 sq km)

Iceland 39,681 sq miles (102,775 sq km)

Ireland 32,595 sq miles (84,421 sq km)

ASIA

Highest mountains

Mt Everest 29,029 ft (8,848 m)

K2 28,251 ft (8,611 m)

Kanchenjunga 28,169 ft (8,586 m)

Longest rivers

Yangtze 3,915 miles (6,300 km)

Yellow 3,395 miles (5,464 km)

Lena 2,734 miles (4,400 km)

Largest islands

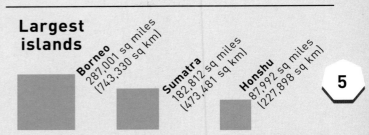

Borneo 287,001 sq miles (743,330 sq km)

Sumatra 182,812 sq miles (473,481 sq km)

Honshu 87,992 sq miles (227,898 sq km)

5

AFRICA

Highest mountains

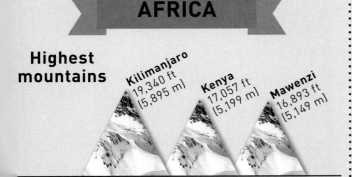

Kilimanjaro 19,340 ft (5,895 m)

Kenya 17,057 ft (5,199 m)

Mawenzi 16,893 ft (5,149 m)

Longest rivers

Nile 4,258 miles (6,853 km)

Congo 2,920 miles (4,700 km)

Niger 2,597 miles (4,180 km)

Largest islands

Madagascar 226,641 sq miles (587,000 sq km)

Socotra 1,465 sq miles (3,796 sq km)

Réunion 374 sq miles (969 sq km)

OCEANIA

Highest mountains

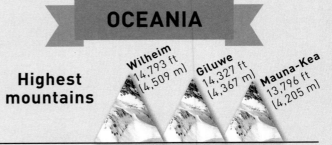

Wilheim 14,793 ft (4,509 m)

Giluwe 14,327 ft (4,367 m)

Mauna-Kea 13,796 ft (4,205 m)

Longest rivers

Murray 1,476 miles (2,375 km)

Murrumbidgee 923 miles (1,485 km)

Darling 915 miles (1,472 km)

Largest islands

New Guinea 178,704 sq miles (462,840 sq km)

New Zealand South island 58,384 sq miles (151,215 sq km)

New Zealand North island 43,911 sq miles (113,729 sq km)

CLIMATE

Regional **climates** around the world vary greatly, partly due to an area's location between the equator and the poles. Climates can be hot or cold, and some areas can get a great deal of rain, while some can get very little. Some areas also have different seasons, where conditions vary from month to month.

WORLD CLIMATE TYPES

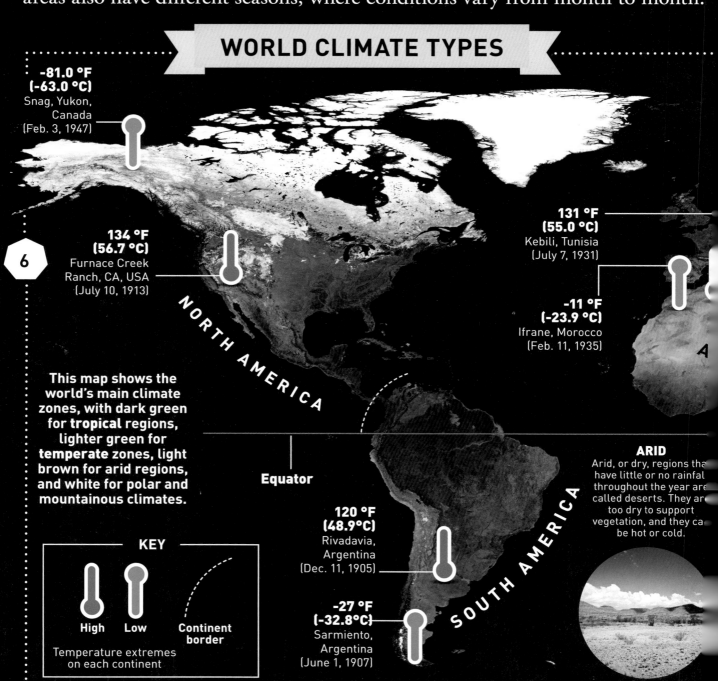

-81.0 °F (-63.0 °C)
Snag, Yukon, Canada
(Feb. 3, 1947)

131 °F (55.0 °C)
Kebili, Tunisia
(July 7, 1931)

134 °F (56.7 °C)
Furnace Creek Ranch, CA, USA
(July 10, 1913)

-11 °F (-23.9 °C)
Ifrane, Morocco
(Feb. 11, 1935)

NORTH AMERICA

This map shows the world's main climate zones, with dark green for tropical regions, lighter green for temperate zones, light brown for arid regions, and white for polar and mountainous climates.

Equator

SOUTH AMERICA

120 °F (48.9°C)
Rivadavia, Argentina
(Dec. 11, 1905)

-27 °F (-32.8°C)
Sarmiento, Argentina
(June 1, 1907)

ARID
Arid, or dry, regions that have little or no rainfall throughout the year are called deserts. They are too dry to support vegetation, and they can be hot or cold.

KEY

High Low Continent border

Temperature extremes on each continent

6

MEDITERRANEAN
Named after the climate around the Mediterranean Sea, this climate is found in parts of the world such as Chile, California, and South Africa. It has warm, dry summers and cool, wet winters.

TEMPERATE
Temperate zones lie midway between the tropics and the poles. They usually have mild summers and winters, and rainfall levels can be high throughout the year.

POLAR
The climates around the poles are cold throughout the year, but especially during the winter months when the Sun may not rise above the horizon. Close to the poles, the sea and the land are covered by thick sheets of ice.

**118.4 °F
(48.0 °C)**
Athens, Greece
(July 19, 1977)

**-72.6 °F
(-58.1 °C)**
Ust-Schuger, Russia
(Dec. 21, 1978)

**-90.04 °F
(-67.8 °C)**
Verkhoyansk and Omkon, Russia
(Feb. 5, 1892, Feb. 7, 1892,
Feb. 6, 1933)

EUROPE

ASIA

**129.2 °F
(54.0 °C)**
Tirat Zvi, Israel
(June 21, 1942)

ICA

7

MOUNTAINS
Highland regions, such as the Andes and the Himalayas, have no distinct seasons. Conditions vary the higher you climb.

TROPICAL
Tropical regions lie on either side of the equator. They can be tropical wet, with high levels of rainfall throughout the year, or tropical dry, with two distinct seasons—a wet season and a dry season.

**123.26 °F
(50.7 °C)**
Oodnadatta,
Australia
(Jan. 2, 1960)

OCEANIA

**-9.4 °F
(-23.0 °C)**
Charlotte Pass, NSW,
Australia (June 29, 1994)

BIODIVERSITY

Some parts of the world, such as rain forests, are home to thousands of different **species** of living things, while others, such as the poles and hot deserts, may only have a handful.

BIODIVERSITY RANGE AND HOTSPOTS

This map shows the countries with the highest and lowest numbers of species. This variation of species is known as the region's **biodiversity**.

KEY

Top 5

Bottom 5

Biodiversity
(total number of amphibian, bird, mammal, reptile, and vascular plant species)

Biodiversity Hotspots
Biodiversity hotspots are areas that have at least 1,500 species of plants, but are under threat because they have lost more than 70 percent of the original plant cover.

Haiti
5,716
species

Portugal
5,714
species

Spain
5,796
species

Mexico
28,836
species

Colombia
54,649
species

Brazil
59,851
species

NUMBER OF SPECIES IN THE WORLD

Thousands of new species are discovered every year, and estimates show that far more species are yet to be found.

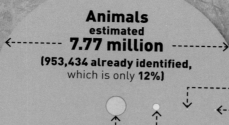

Animals estimated **7.77 million** (953,434 already identified, which is only **12%**)

Protozoa estimated **36,400** (8,118 already identified which is only **22%**)

Fungi estimated **611,000** (43,271 already identified which is only **7%**)

Plants estimated **298,000** (215,644 already identified which is only **72%**)

Algae estimated **27,500** (13,033 already identified which is only **47%**)

TOTAL ESTIMATE **8.74 MILLION** SPECIES ON PLANET EARTH

China 34,687 species

Indonesia 32,680 species

Pakistan 5,977 species

Bangladesh 5,871 species

FORESTS

The world's forests are not evenly distributed around the globe—two thirds of them lie in just 10 countries: Russia, Brazil, Canada, the United States, China, Australia, the Democratic Republic of the Congo, Indonesia, Peru, and India. However, these forests are under threat as trees are cut down for fuel or to make way for farms and towns.

DEFORESTATION AND REFORESTATION

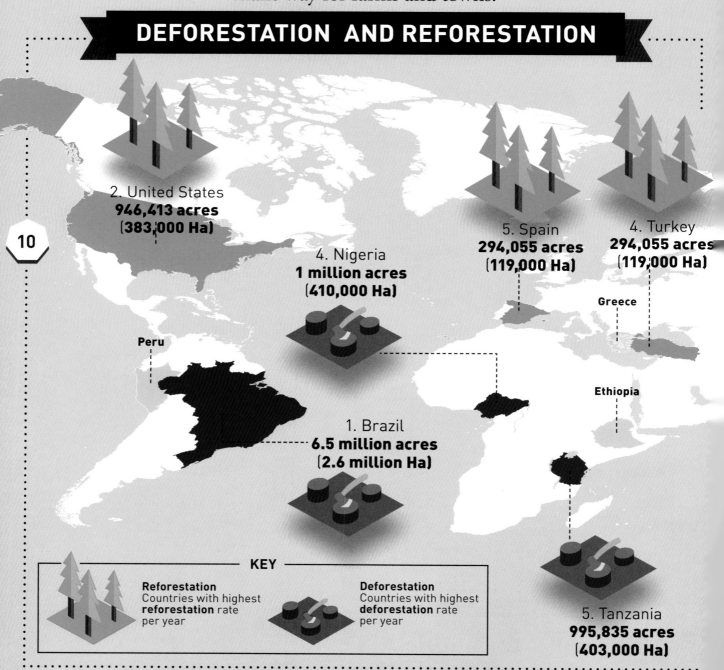

2. United States
946,413 acres
(383,000 Ha)

4. Nigeria
1 million acres
(410,000 Ha)

5. Spain
294,055 acres
(119,000 Ha)

4. Turkey
294,055 acres
(119,000 Ha)

Greece

Peru

Ethiopia

1. Brazil
6.5 million acres
(2.6 million Ha)

KEY

Reforestation
Countries with highest **reforestation** rate per year

Deforestation
Countries with highest **deforestation** rate per year

5. Tanzania
995,835 acres
(403,000 Ha)

2.47 ACRES (1 HECTARE) of trees will produce enough oxygen for

45 people to breathe in a year

THE AMAZONIAN RAIN FOREST ALONE PRODUCES ABOUT **20 PERCENT** OF THE WORLD'S OXYGEN.

REFORESTATION

The Bonn Challenge asks countries to commit to restoring 370.7 million acres (150 million Ha) of forest by 2020—an area larger than Peru.

20%

The biggest commitment to reforestation has been made by **Ethiopia**. The country has pledged to restore **54.4 million acres (22 million Ha)** of forest, which is more than 20 percent of its land area.

Global deforestation rate

In total, nearly **32 million acres (13 million Ha)** of forest are lost each year. This is an area equivalent to the size of Greece.

11

1. China
7.4 million acres (3 million Ha)

3. Vietnam
511,508 acres (207,000 Ha)

3. Indonesia
1.2 million acres (498,000 Ha)

2. Australia
1.4 million acres (562,000 Ha)

RARE SPECIES

One of the rarest species in the world is the Wollemi pine. It was thought to be extinct until about 100 trees were discovered in a remote valley near Sydney, Australia, in 1994. The species is at least 200 million years old.

DESERTS

A desert is a region that receives less than 10 inches (25 cm) of precipitation per year. Deserts cover about one third of Earth's land area, and they can be hot or cold. They are covered in sand, rocks, or ice sheets.

MAJOR DESERTS

Great Basin
North America
189,190 sq miles
(490,000 sq km)

7

12

Chihuahuan
Mexico
174,904 sq miles
(453,000 sq km)

9

GREAT DUNE OF PYLA, ARCACHON BAY
France
351 feet (107 m)
Tallest sand dune in Europe

ISAOUANE-N-TIFERNINE SAND SEA
Algeria
1,411 feet (430 m)
Tallest sand dunes in Africa

Sahara
Africa
3.5 million sq mil
(9.1 million sq km

DUNA FEDERICO KIRBUS
Argentina
4,035 feet (1,230 m)
Tallest sand dune in the world

5

Patagonian
South America
258,688 sq miles
(670,000 sq km)

KEY

Major Deserts
The world's major deserts and their sizes

Danger of desertification
These regions are usually found next to existing deserts and are at risk of desertification, or becoming deserts themselves.

Tallest sand dunes
Dunes are created when wind blows over large areas of sand, creating waves, or dunes, some of which can be hundreds of feet high.

Singing Sand

Singing sand can sometimes be heard in a desert when a surface layer of sand flows down a dune. This can happen if someone walks near the top of a dune and disturbs the sand, or if a strong wind moves it. The noise can be a low boom or a shrill squeak with a volume of up to 105 **decibels**—as loud as a revving snowmobile engine.

Syrian
Arabian Peninsula
189,190 sq miles
(490,000 sq km)

Gobi
China and Mongolia
501,933 sq miles
(1,300,000 sq km)

4

8

13

BADAIN JARAN DUNES
China
**1,640 feet
(500 m)**
Tallest sand dunes in Asia

2

3

Arabian
Arabian Peninsula
1 million sq miles
(2.6 million sq km)

Great Victoria
Australia
249,808 sq miles
(647,000 sq km)

6

7

Kalahari
Africa
220,078 sq miles
(570,000 sq km)

Antarctic
Antarctica
5.5 million sq miles
(14 million sq km)

**MOUNT TEMPEST,
MORETON ISLAND**
Australia
935 feet (285 m)
Tallest coastal sand dune

1

Adapting for SURVIVAL

Around the world, different animals have **evolved**, or developed certain characteristics, to survive in their environment. This can include thick fur to stay warm in the polar chill, or a super-long neck to grasp food that is out of reach for most other animals.

ANIMAL HABITATS

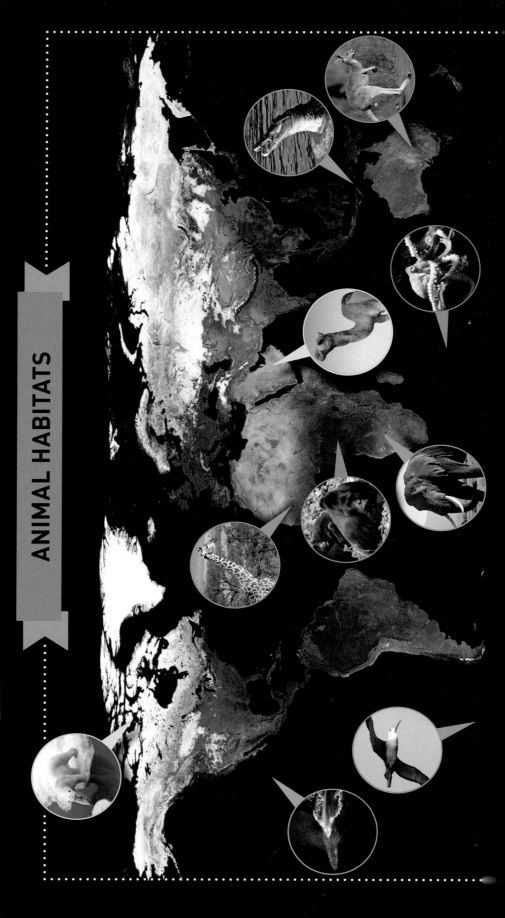

Wandering albatross

RANGE
SOUTHERN OCEAN

Albatrosses have long, thin wings, which they use to catch ocean winds and glide for hours on end without even a single flap.

Blue whale

RANGE
ALL OCEANS

The largest animal that has ever lived is able to grow to an enormous size because its body weight is supported by water. Its mouth is filled with large frills called baleen plates. The whale feeds on krill and zooplankton by lunging and opening its mouth. The excess water is squeezed out through the baleen.

Camels

RANGE
AFRICA, MIDDLE EAST, AND SOUTH ASIA.

Camels have adapted to life in dry desert climates. They have long eyelashes to keep sand out of their eyes and they can close their nostrils to keep sand out of their noses. Their humps are full of fat and act as a food store, and they have huge feet so that they don't sink into the sand.

Kangaroos

RANGE
AUSTRALIA

Kangaroos have long, powerful legs, which they use to bound across the open grasslands of Australia.

Polar bears

RANGE
ARCTIC

Polar bears have thick fur and a layer of fat to keep them warm in the freezing Arctic. They can also swim for many miles from one patch of sea ice to another in search of prey.

Octopus

RANGE
ALL OCEANS

This mollusk does not have an internal skeleton. This means that it can squeeze its body into tiny cracks to hide from predators or to search for prey.

African elephant

RANGE
AFRICA

The largest land animal on the planet has huge ears, which it uses to control its body heat. Its long trunk is used to pick up food and objects, scoop up water, sniff things, and to feel and communicate with other elephants.

Giraffes

RANGE
AFRICA

Giraffes use their long necks to reach leaves high up in trees and out of reach of other animals' grasp. They are also able to spot faraway predators. They have strong hearts to push blood up to their heads.

Gorillas

RANGE
AFRICA

Gorillas have thick fur to protect their skin from biting insects and to keep them warm. They have large teeth to help them chew the plants and leaves that make up their diet.

Saltwater crocodiles

RANGE
EASTERN INDIA, SOUTHEAST ASIA, AND NORTHERN AUSTRALIA

These huge reptiles use their enormous size to ambush and overpower prey. They have powerful tails to push themselves through the water. Their eyes and noses are on top of their heads so they can remain submerged and out of sight of their unsuspecting prey.

15

Animal MIGRATION

Many animals take part in regular journeys in search of food or water, or to find somewhere to give birth and raise their young. These journeys, called **migrations**, can cover thousands of miles or just a few hundred feet.

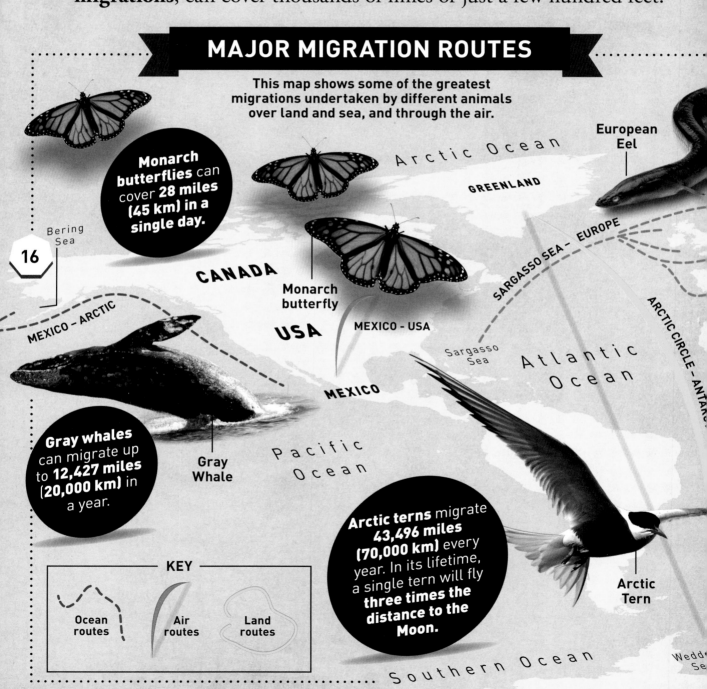

MAJOR MIGRATION ROUTES

This map shows some of the greatest migrations undertaken by different animals over land and sea, and through the air.

Arctic Ocean

GREENLAND

European Eel

Monarch butterflies can cover **28 miles (45 km)** in a single day.

Bering Sea

SARGASSO SEA – EUROPE

ARCTIC CIRCLE – ANTARCTICA

CANADA

Monarch butterfly

MEXICO – ARCTIC

USA

MEXICO – USA

Sargasso Sea

Atlantic Ocean

MEXICO

Gray whales can migrate up to **12,427 miles (20,000 km)** in a year.

Gray Whale

Pacific Ocean

Arctic terns migrate **43,496 miles (70,000 km)** every year. In its lifetime, a single tern will fly **three times the distance to the Moon.**

Arctic Tern

KEY

Ocean routes

Air routes

Land routes

Southern Ocean

Weddell Sea

ZOOPLANKTON

Every night, huge numbers of tiny animals called zooplankton (right), travel hundreds of feet up toward the ocean surface for food, then down to deeper water in the morning to hide, in a movement called vertical migration.

Wandering glider dragonflies migrate by using fast-moving winds that blow **at altitudes of nearly 4 miles (6.5 km).**

A single leatherback turtle swam more than **12,738 miles (20,500 km) from Indonesia to the United States** in 2003.

A European eel migrates to breed and lays up to **10 million eggs at a time.**

Wandering glider dragonfly

Leatherback Turtle

17

Wildebeest

INDIA

INDIA – AFRICA

Indian Ocean

INDONESIA

CHRISTMAS ISLAND

AUSTRALIA

KENYA

TANZANIA

Nearly **1.5 million wildebeest** take part in the **largest yearly land migration on the planet.**

Red crab

On Christmas Island near Indonesia, nearly **50 million red crabs** migrate to the sea at the same time to lay eggs.

ANTARCTICA

Endangered SPECIES

Scientists believe that more than 20,000 species of plants and animals are on the brink of extinction. This includes about one third of all amphibian species, a quarter of the world's mammals, and an eighth of all bird species.

THREATENED SPECIES

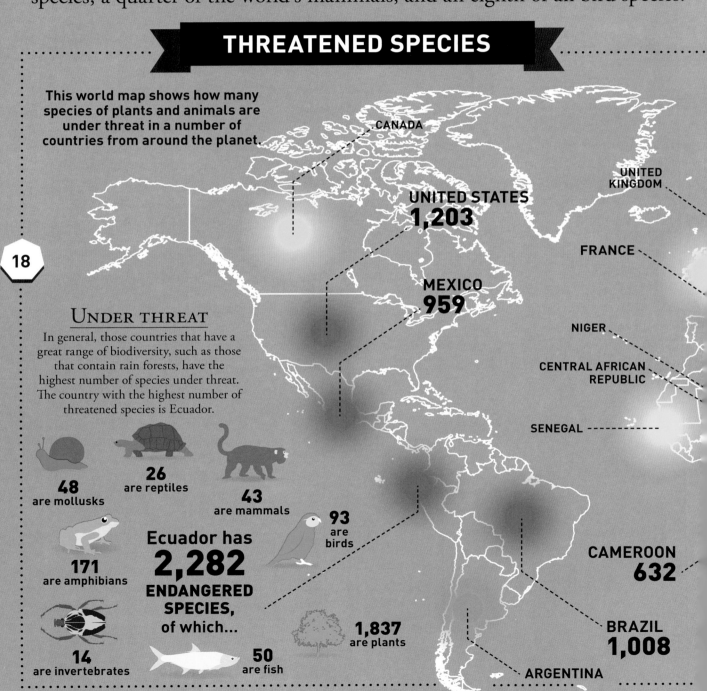

This world map shows how many species of plants and animals are under threat in a number of countries from around the planet.

CANADA

UNITED STATES
1,203

MEXICO
959

UNITED KINGDOM

FRANCE

NIGER

CENTRAL AFRICAN REPUBLIC

SENEGAL

CAMEROON
632

BRAZIL
1,008

ARGENTINA

UNDER THREAT

In general, those countries that have a great range of biodiversity, such as those that contain rain forests, have the highest number of species under threat. The country with the highest number of threatened species is Ecuador.

48 are mollusks

26 are reptiles

43 are mammals

171 are amphibians

Ecuador has **2,282** ENDANGERED SPECIES, of which...

93 are birds

14 are invertebrates

50 are fish

1,837 are plants

WHY DO SPECIES BECOME ENDANGERED?

There are many reasons why plant and animal species become **endangered**. Some species are worth a lot of money and are collected or hunted, while other species are threatened by pollution and disease. Some of the greatest threats come from habitat loss, climate change, and the appearance of foreign species.

Habitat loss
Habitat destruction, such as the clearing of forests for mines or cities, reduces the area a species lives in, as well as its food supply.

Climate change
A change in a region's climate can destroy a habitat and reduce the amount of food sources, making it difficult for a species to survive.

Invasive species
A new, foreign species may compete for the same food as a native species, or it can even feed on the native species, reducing its numbers.

KEY
Number of threatened species
(plants and animals) in selected countries:

High
500 species and above

Medium
between 100–500 species

Low
fewer than 100 species

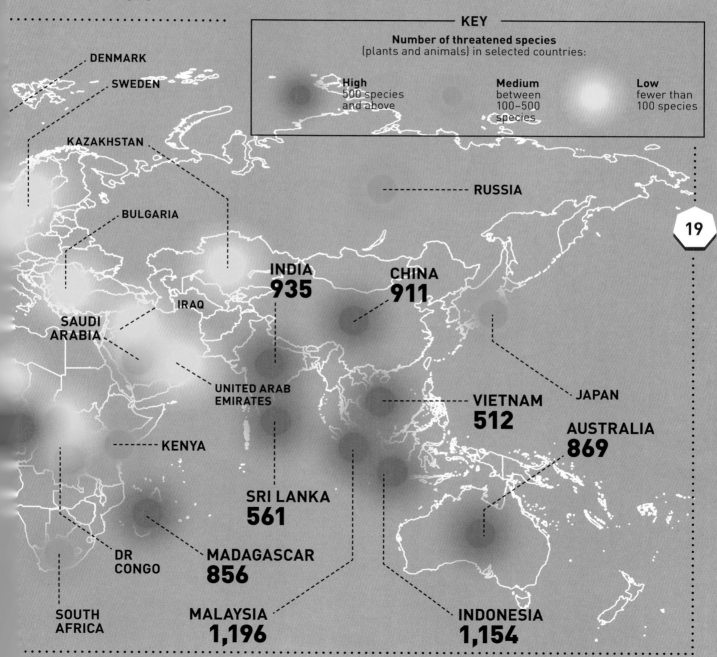

DENMARK

SWEDEN

KAZAKHSTAN

RUSSIA

BULGARIA

19

INDIA
935

CHINA
911

IRAQ

SAUDI ARABIA

JAPAN

UNITED ARAB EMIRATES

VIETNAM
512

AUSTRALIA
869

KENYA

SRI LANKA
561

DR CONGO

MADAGASCAR
856

SOUTH AFRICA

MALAYSIA
1,196

INDONESIA
1,154

OCEANS

Earth's oceans are vast, and we have only explored less than five percent of them. Beneath the surface are thousands of undiscovered species, as well as physical features such as volcanoes, canyons, and mountain ridges.

THE WORLD'S OCEANS

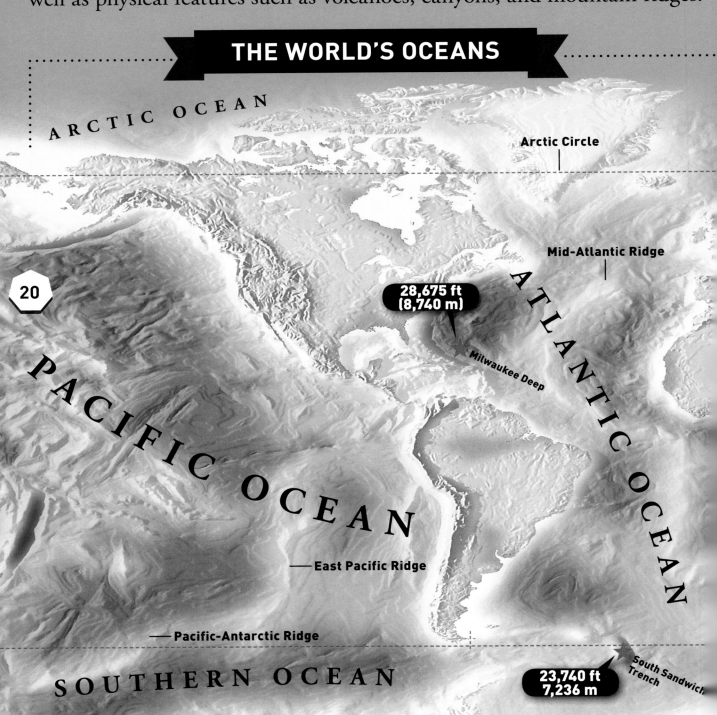

ARCTIC OCEAN

Arctic Circle

Mid-Atlantic Ridge

28,675 ft (8,740 m)

Milwaukee Deep

ATLANTIC OCEAN

PACIFIC OCEAN

East Pacific Ridge

Pacific-Antarctic Ridge

South Sandwich Trench

23,740 ft 7,236 m

SOUTHERN OCEAN

ANTARCTICA

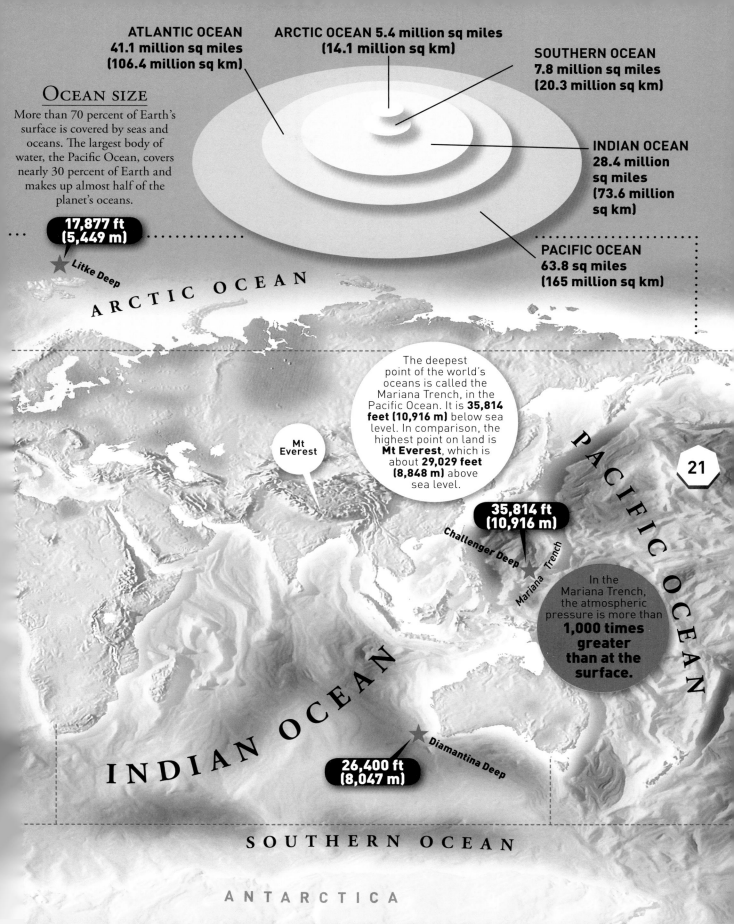

OCEAN SIZE

More than 70 percent of Earth's surface is covered by seas and oceans. The largest body of water, the Pacific Ocean, covers nearly 30 percent of Earth and makes up almost half of the planet's oceans.

ATLANTIC OCEAN 41.1 million sq miles (106.4 million sq km)

ARCTIC OCEAN 5.4 million sq miles (14.1 million sq km)

SOUTHERN OCEAN 7.8 million sq miles (20.3 million sq km)

INDIAN OCEAN 28.4 million sq miles (73.6 million sq km)

PACIFIC OCEAN 63.8 sq miles (165 million sq km)

17,877 ft (5,449 m)

★ Litke Deep

ARCTIC OCEAN

The deepest point of the world's oceans is called the Mariana Trench, in the Pacific Ocean. It is **35,814 feet (10,916 m)** below sea level. In comparison, the highest point on land is **Mt Everest**, which is about **29,029 feet (8,848 m)** above sea level.

Mt Everest

PACIFIC OCEAN

21

35,814 ft (10,916 m)

Challenger Deep

Mariana Trench

In the Mariana Trench, the atmospheric pressure is more than **1,000 times greater than at the surface.**

INDIAN OCEAN

★ Diamantina Deep

26,400 ft (8,047 m)

SOUTHERN OCEAN

ANTARCTICA

Plates and QUAKES

Earth's crust is split up into huge blocks called **tectonic plates**. These plates move very slowly, crashing into each other and scraping together or pulling apart. This action triggers powerful and devastating earthquakes.

TECTONIC PLATES

This map shows the world's tectonic plates, the direction in which they are moving, and the locations of the most powerful and deadliest earthquakes.

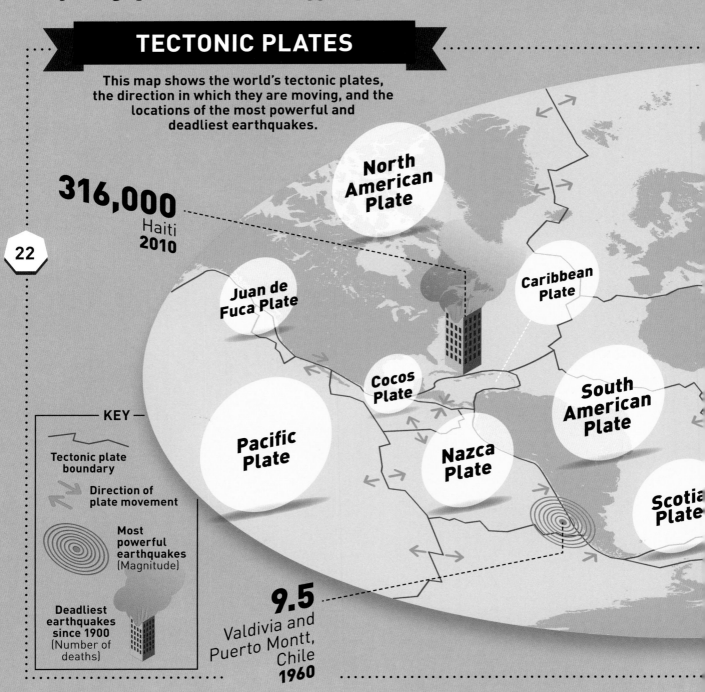

316,000
Haiti
2010

North American Plate

Caribbean Plate

Juan de Fuca Plate

Cocos Plate

South American Plate

Pacific Plate

Nazca Plate

Scotia Plate

KEY

Tectonic plate boundary

Direction of plate movement

Most powerful earthquakes
(Magnitude)

Deadliest earthquakes since 1900
(Number of deaths)

9.5
Valdivia and Puerto Montt, Chile
1960

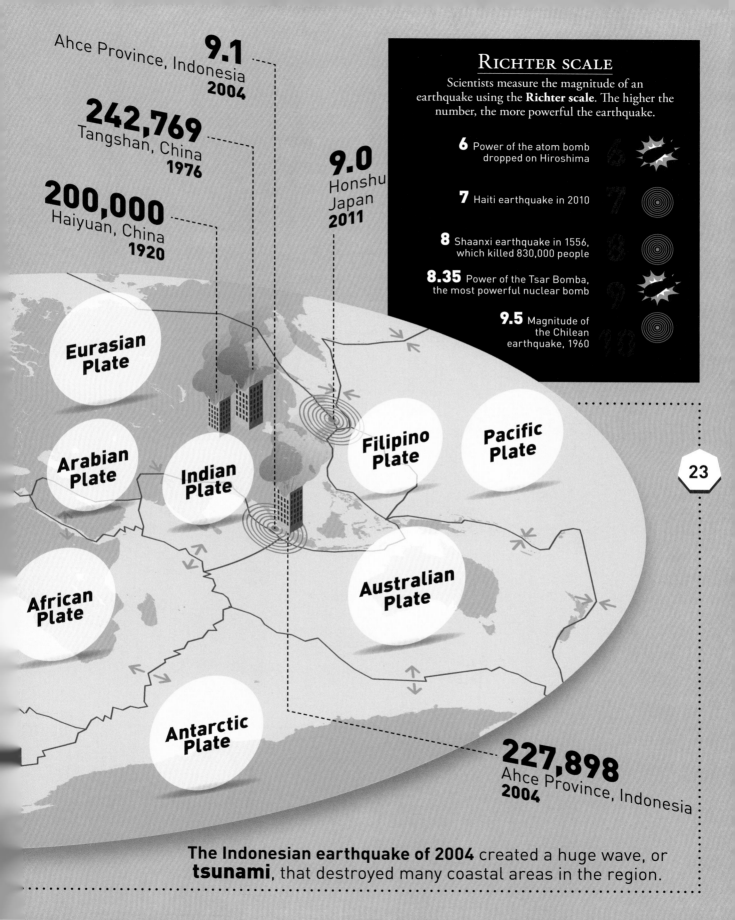

9.1
Ahce Province, Indonesia
2004

242,769
Tangshan, China
1976

200,000
Haiyuan, China
1920

9.0
Honshu
Japan
2011

RICHTER SCALE

Scientists measure the magnitude of an earthquake using the **Richter scale**. The higher the number, the more powerful the earthquake.

6 Power of the atom bomb dropped on Hiroshima

7 Haiti earthquake in 2010

8 Shaanxi earthquake in 1556, which killed 830,000 people

8.35 Power of the Tsar Bomba, the most powerful nuclear bomb

9.5 Magnitude of the Chilean earthquake, 1960

Eurasian Plate

Arabian Plate

Indian Plate

Filipino Plate

Pacific Plate

African Plate

Australian Plate

Antarctic Plate

227,898
Ahce Province, Indonesia
2004

The Indonesian earthquake of 2004 created a huge wave, or **tsunami**, that destroyed many coastal areas in the region.

VOLCANOES

Volcanoes are holes in Earth's crust through which super-hot molten rock, or **lava**, pours out of the ground. Most of them are found around the edges of Earth's tectonic plates, but some are found in the middle of a plate, where the rock is thin enough for lava to erupt.

ACTIVE VOLCANOES

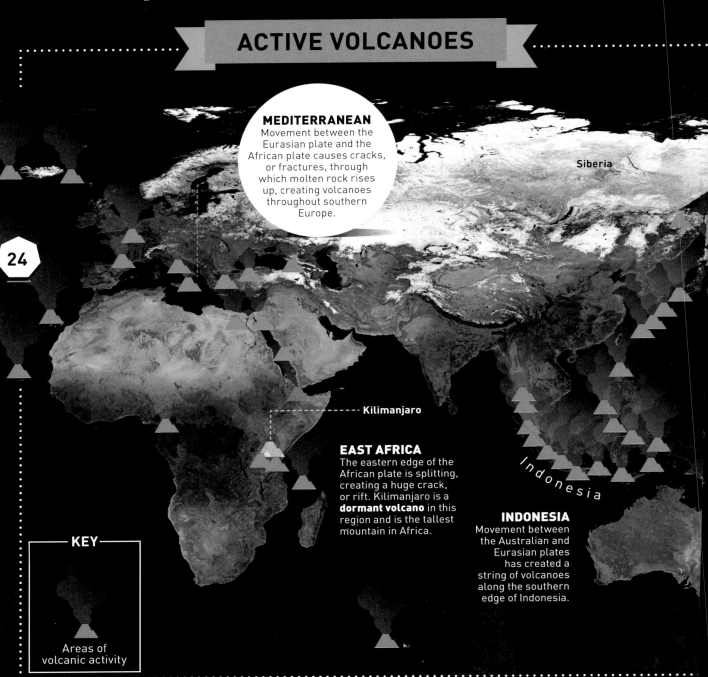

MEDITERRANEAN
Movement between the Eurasian plate and the African plate causes cracks, or fractures, through which molten rock rises up, creating volcanoes throughout southern Europe.

Siberia

Kilimanjaro

EAST AFRICA
The eastern edge of the African plate is splitting, creating a huge crack, or rift. Kilimanjaro is a **dormant volcano** in this region and is the tallest mountain in Africa.

Indonesia

INDONESIA
Movement between the Australian and Eurasian plates has created a string of volcanoes along the southern edge of Indonesia.

KEY

Areas of volcanic activity

DIFFERENT TYPES OF VOLCANO

Caldera
A large crater or bowl that is formed when land collapses during an eruption

Shield
Formed by runny lava, which hardens to create a large volcano with a low profile

Dome
Formed by thick lava, which hardens to create a circular mound

Composite
Also known as a stratovolcano, this is formed by layers of lava, rock and ash that build up over a number of eruptions

Ring of Fire

YELLOWSTONE
Beneath the Yellowstone National Park is one of the biggest volcanoes on the planet. This supervolcano last erupted more than 600,000 years ago.

ALASKA
Tectonic activity in the northern Pacific has created a string of volcanoes that stretch from Alaska to Siberia.

EASTERN PACIFIC
The ring of volcanoes around the Pacific Ocean is known as the Pacific Ring of Fire. The eastern edge of this ring is created by movement between the Pacific, Filipino, and North American plates.

Yellowstone
National
Park

HAWAII
The Hawaiian volcanoes are found in the middle of the Pacific plate, far away from any plate boundaries. There, the plate is so thin that it creates a hotspot where volcanoes are formed.

There are more than

1,500

active volcanoes around the world. An active volcano is one that has erupted within the last 10,000 years.

New Zealand

ANDES
The volcanoes of the Andes are formed by the Nazca plate being pushed beneath the South American plate as the two plates crash into each other.

Natural
DISASTERS

Regular seasonal extremes of rainfall and temperature create severe storms that lash regions and cause great damage. Other deadly disasters include avalanches and large earthquake-created tsunamis.

THE WORST DISASTERS

United States
June–August 1980
temp. highs of
104 °F (40 °C)
**up to 5,000
fatalities**

Tyrolean Alps avalanche
Italy, 1916
10,000 fatalities

Europe
June–August 2003,
temp. highs of 116.6 °F (47 °C)
70,000 fatalities

Hurricane Mitch
Central America/
Florida, 1998
**11,000
fatalities**

**Huascaran
avalanche**
Peru, 1970
**20,000
fatalities**

**Huascaran
avalanche**
Peru, 1962
4,000 fatalities

**Great Lisbon
Earthquake**
Lisbon, Portugal,
November 1755
waves 65.6 ft (20 m) high
**more than
60,000 fatalities**

Indonesia
December 2004
waves 98 ft (30 m) high
227,898 fatalities

Krakatoa Volcano
Indonesia, August 1883
waves 131 ft (40 m) high
36,000 fatalities

KEY

**Deadliest
typhoons and
hurricanes**

**Deadliest
heatwaves**

**Deadliest
tsunamis**

**Deadliest
avalanches**

DEADLY EVENTS

As well as the four events shown here, natural disasters can include earthquakes, volcanic eruptions, floods, blizzards, **droughts**, tornadoes, wildfires, and even meteorite impacts.

Typhoons and Hurricanes
Massive swirling storms called hurricanes, cyclones, or typhoons can measure hundreds of miles across.

Avalanches
Huge slides of snow that crash down mountain slopes are known as avalanches. They can travel at speeds of up to 249 mph (400 kph).

Heatwaves
Prolonged periods of high temperatures are called heatwaves. They can trigger fires and can be dangerous to vulnerable people, such as the elderly and very young.

Tsunamis
These are enormous waves that are usually triggered by earthquakes and underwater volcanic eruptions. These waves rush ashore and destroy everything in their path, before sweeping back out to sea.

Russia
July–September 2010
temp. highs of 111.2 °F (44 °C)
56,000 fatalities

India
May–June 2003,
temp. highs of 95 °F (35 °C)
1,500 fatalities

Bhola Cyclone
Bangladesh, 1970
500,000 fatalities

Bangladesh Cyclone
Bangladesh, 1991
138,366 fatalities

Japan
July–September 2010
temp. highs of 95 °F (35 °C)
1,718 fatalities

Super Typhoon Nina
China, 1975
229,000 fatalities

Cyclone Nargis
Myanmar, 2008
138,366 fatalities

Japan
September 1498
waves estimated to be:
33–66 ft (10–20 m) high
31,000 fatalities

Japan
March 2011
waves 33 ft (10 m) high
18,000 fatalities

27

Climate CHANGE

Throughout its history, Earth's temperatures have varied, creating ice ages and warmer periods. Scientists predict that global temperatures could rise as much as 10 °F (5.6 °C) over the next century. This would have dramatic effect

RISING SEA LEVELS

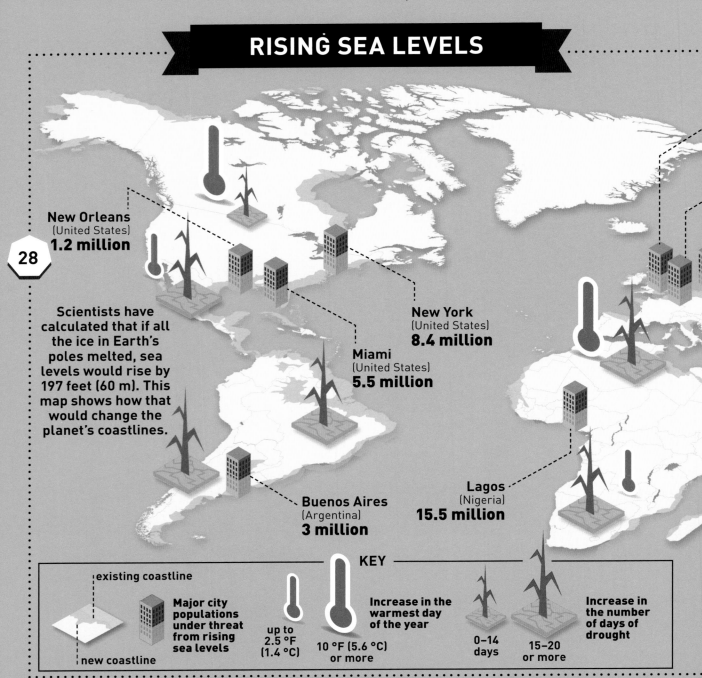

New Orleans
(United States)
1.2 million

Scientists have calculated that if all the ice in Earth's poles melted, sea levels would rise by 197 feet (60 m). This map shows how that would change the planet's coastlines.

New York
(United States)
8.4 million

Miami
(United States)
5.5 million

Buenos Aires
(Argentina)
3 million

Lagos
(Nigeria)
15.5 million

KEY

existing coastline

new coastline

Major city populations under threat from rising sea levels

up to 2.5 °F (1.4 °C)

10 °F (5.6 °C) or more

Increase in the warmest day of the year

0–14 days

15–20 or more

Increase in the number of days of drought

COSTS TO MAJOR CITIES IF SEA LEVELS RISE

Miami $3.5 trillion
Guangzhou (China) $3.4 trillion
New York $2.1 trillion
Kolkata (India) $2 trillion
Shanghai (China) $1.8 trillion

DROUGHT

A drought is when a region experiences below-average rainfall for an extended period of time. Droughts can cause crops to fail, leading to famine. The worst famine in history occurred in 1876–1879 in northern China when there was little rainfall for three years, resulting in 9–13 million deaths.

London (United Kingdom)
3.6 million

Amsterdam (Netherlands)
1.6 million

Copenhagen (Denmark)
1.9 million

Kolkata (India)
11.8 million

Dhaka
(Bangladesh)
17.5 million

Shanghai
(China)
23.9 million

Tokyo
(Japan)
37.8 million

Mumbai
(India)
21 million

Guangzhou
(China)
10.3 million

Ho Chi Minh City
(Vietnam)
9.2 million

Hong Kong
(China)
7.2 million

—Mapping the— WORLD

The maps in this book are two-dimensional representations of our sphere-shaped world. Maps allow us to display a huge range of information, including the size of the countries and where people live.

Projections

Converting the three-dimensional world into a two-dimensional map can produce different views, called projections. These projections can show different areas of the Earth.

GLOBE
Earth is shaped like a sphere, with the landmasses wrapped around it.

CURVED
Some maps show parts of the world as they would appear on this ball.

FLAT
Maps of the whole world show the landmasses laid out flat. The maps in this book use projections like this.

Types of maps

Different types of maps can show different types of information. Physical maps show physical features, such as mountains and rivers, while political maps show countries and cities. Schematic maps show specific types of information, such as routes on a city subway network, and they may not necessarily show things in exactly the right place.

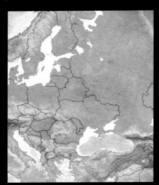

Physical map

Political map

Schematic map

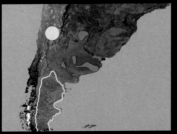

Colored regions

Scaled symbols

Map symbols

Maps use many symbols to show information, such as blue lines for rivers and colors for different regions. Some of the symbols in this book show the locations of subjects, or the symbols are different sizes to represent different values—the bigger the symbol, the greater the value.

GLOSSARY

BIODIVERSITY
The number and range of different plant and animal species that live in a region

CLIMATE
The long-term weather conditions that a region experiences; climate can be affected by how close a region is to the equator, physical features such as mountains, and how close it is to the ocean

CONTINENT
One of seven large land masses that make up Earth's land surface

DECIBELS
A unit used to measure the intensity, or loudness, of a sound

DEFORESTATION
The clearing of large areas of forest, usually to make way for farms, mines, or urban areas

DESERTIFICATION
When regions become deserts

DORMANT VOLCANO
A type of volcano that has not erupted for a long period of time, but could still erupt in the future

DROUGHT
An extended period when very little or no rain falls

ENDANGERED
When the numbers of a species have become so low, that it is in danger of becoming extinct

EVOLVE
To develop gradually, especially from a simple to a complex form

LAVA
Molten rock that has reached Earth's surface during a volcanic eruption

MIGRATION
The movement of animals to a new area, usually in search of food, water, a mate, or a suitable place to raise young

REFORESTATION
The planting of new forests to replace those that have been cut down

RICHTER SCALE
The scale used to measure the strength of an earthquake

SPECIES
A group of living things that are very similar to each other, and can reproduce with each other and produce fertile offspring

TECTONIC PLATES
The large pieces of Earth's surface that fit together to form the crust

TEMPERATE
Describes a region that is midway between the equator and the poles; temperate regions have mild weather conditions

TROPICAL
Used to describe a region that lies on either side of the equator; tropical regions have warm weather conditions

TSUNAMI
A large wave caused by an underwater earthquake or volcanic eruption

WEBSITES

www.nationalgeographic.com/kids-world-atlas/maps.html
The map section of the National Geographic website where readers can create their own maps and study maps covering different topics.

www.mapsofworld.com/kids/
Website with a comprehensive collection of maps covering a wide range of themes that are aimed at students and available to download and print out.

www.cia.gov/library/publications/resources/the-world-factbook/
The information resource for the Central Intelligence Agency (CIA), this offers detailed facts and figures on a range of topics, such as population and transportation, about every single country in the world.

www.kids-world-travel-guide.com
Website with facts and travel tips about a host of countries from around the world.

INDEX